LET'S INVESTIGATE
Area and Volume

LET'S INVESTIGATE
Area
and Volume

By Marion Smoothey
Illustrated by Ted Evans

MARSHALL CAVENDISH
NEW YORK · LONDON · TORONTO · SYDNEY

Library Edition Published 1993

© Marshall Cavendish Corporation 1993

Published by Marshall Cavendish Corporation
2415 Jerusalem Avenue
PO Box 587
North Bellmore
New York 11710

Series created by Graham Beehag Book Design

Library of Congress Cataloging-in-Publication Data

Smoothey, Marion, 1943-
    Area and Volume / by Marion Smoothey; illustrated by Ted Evans.
        p. cm.. -- (Let's Investigate)
    Includes index.
    Summary: Uses problems and activities to introduce basic mathematical concepts related to area and volume.
    ISBN 1-85435-460-4 ISBN 1-85435-455-8 (set)
    1. Area measurement -- Juvenile literature. 2. Volume (Cubic content)
    [1. Geometry. 2. Area measurement. 3. Volume (Cubic content)
    4. Mathematical recreations.] I. Evans, Ted ill. II. Title. III. Series:
    Smoothey, Marion, 1943- Let's Investigate.
    QA465.563 1992   92-10579
    516.2---dc20   CIP
                                                            AC

Printed in Singapore by Times Offset PTE Ltd
Bound in the United States

Contents

Comparing Areas   7
Same Area, Different Shape   13
Using Squares to Measure Area   15
Calculating the Area of Rectangles   19
Improving the Odds   20
Calculating the Areas of Parallelograms   27
Panels and Pens   31
Calculating the Area of Triangles   37
Calculating the Area of Awkward Shapes   41
Filling Space   46
Boxes and Cubes   50
Calculating Volumes   52
Unit Cubes   56
Surface Area and Volume   59
Enlargement and Area and Volume   60

Glossary   61
Answers   62
Index   64

Look around at the price tags and product labels in a hardware store. You will see many examples of objects and materials which are sold according to the **area** they cover.

Comparing Areas

- Which of these shapes is the smallest?
- Which is the largest?
- Put them in order from the smallest to the largest.

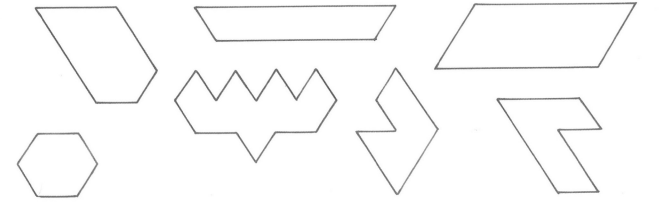

It is easier to compare the sizes of things if you split them all up into smaller equal sized pieces which you can count.

You can divide the shapes on the previous page into equal sized triangles and then count the triangles to see which shape is the largest or smallest.

Check to see if your estimates are correct.

8

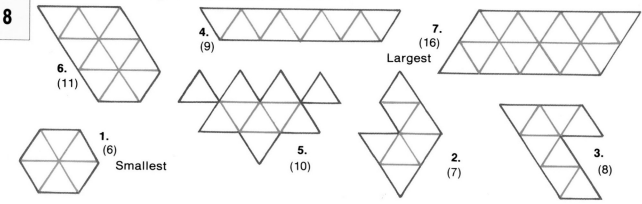

6.
(11)

4.
(9)

7.
(16)
Largest

1.
(6)
Smallest

5.
(10)

2.
(7)

3.
(8)

◇ Not all shapes have straight edges which you can use to make smaller shapes. Which of these pools has the greatest water surface?

One way of making it easier to estimate which pool is the biggest is to draw a pattern of evenly spaced dots inside the shapes and then count the dots. You have to decide whether or not to count the dots on the edges of the pools.

You can also divide each pool into smaller equal shapes and count only the small shapes that are completely inside the pool.

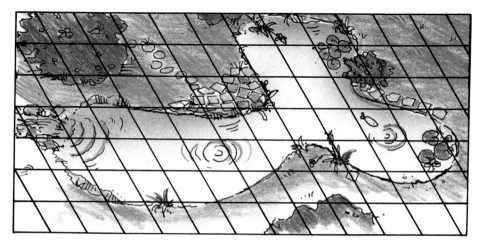

These small shapes are rhombuses.

If you count only the whole rhombuses, you will miss many parts of the pools. Some of the parts are more than half of a rhombus, some are less. If you count half, or more than half, of a rhombus as one, and ignore all the parts that are less than half of a rhombus, you will get a reasonably accurate estimate of how many rhombuses all the parts make.

Transparent grids

You can save time by drawing grids on tracing paper. All you need to do then is lay the tracing paper over the shapes to compare their areas. You can trace these grids and use them to arrange the pools in order of size. Try all three methods of comparing area.

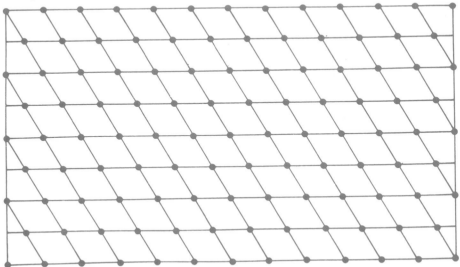

● Does it make any difference, in this case, which method you use?

● Which method do you think gives the most accurate result?

● Greg Smith, the builder, charges according to how many slabs he has to lay when he makes a patio. Which of these patios would be the most expensive? Which would be the cheapest?
If you find it difficult to estimate this, turn to the next page.

11

You can tell much more easily with the slabs drawn in.

1.
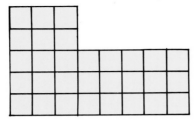

2.
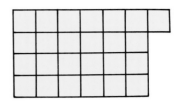

12

3.
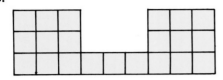

4.
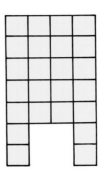

5.
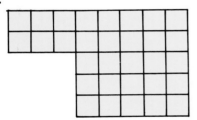

6.
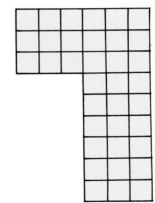

7.
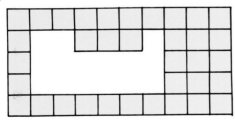

● The cost of laying one slab is $40. How much will each patio cost?

HexaQuilts produces handmade cotton quilts. They charge $20 for each **complete hexagon** and for each part of a hexagon which is a half or more.

● How much will these quilts cost?

King Size

Single

Same Area, Different Shape

13

Three Puzzles

1. How many squares are there in each of these these shapes? Note that two triangles make up one square.

● Which shape has the largest area?

2. Cut out three squares, each with sides of 3″. Leave one whole and cut the other two on the diagonal.

● Join the two cut pieces of each square to form a new shape. What do you know about the area of the new shapes and the area of the un-cut square?

3. Cut out six identical rectangles. Cut five of them in half with a **diagonal** line

● Join each pair of pieces to make a new shape. What are the names of the new shapes? What can you say about the area of all five shapes?

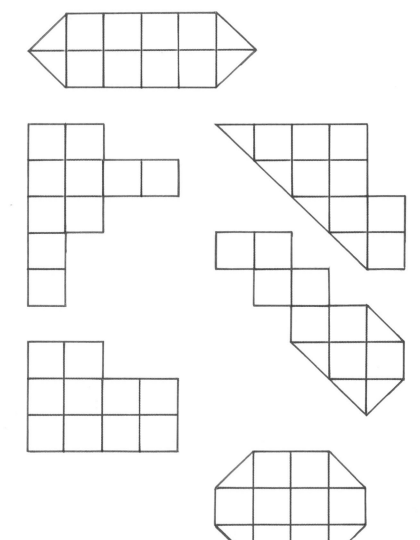

Investigation

Copy these shapes exactly on to thick paper or cardboard. Cut them out. How many different shapes can you make by joining the pieces so that equal sides are together? Draw around your shapes to record your results.

14

● What can you say about the area of each shape you make and the combined area of the three original shapes?

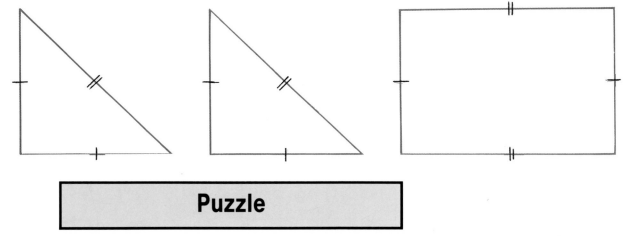

Puzzle

Five of these shapes have the same area. Which is the odd one out?

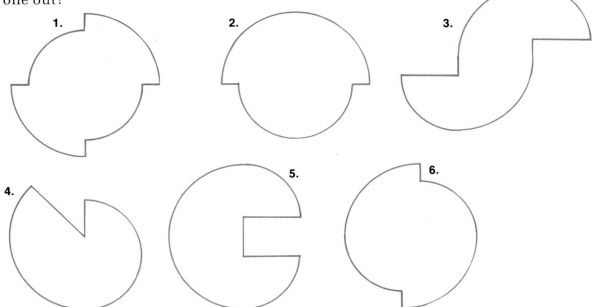

Using Squares to Measure Area

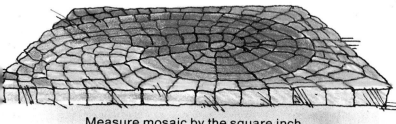

Measure mosaic by the square inch.

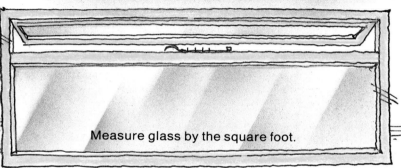

Measure glass by the square foot.

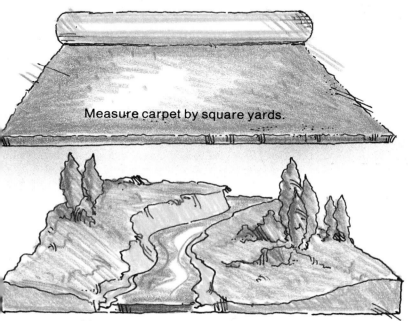

Measure carpet by square yards.

Measure land areas by square miles.

You can measure area using any shape you like. We have already used paving slabs, hexagon patterns, rhombuses, triangles, rectangles and a pattern of dots.

You can measure how much carpet you need to cover the floor of a room by counting how many sheets of newspaper would cover the floor, taking the newspaper to the store and laying it out on the roll of carpet until you get to the right size.

This would not be very convenient. Over the centuries, people have agreed on units of area in just the same way as they have agreed to use yards, feet and inches to measure length or hours, minutes and seconds to measure time. The basic units for measuring area are based on the square. It fits into shapes easily and is easy to count and calculate with.

The squares used have sides of 1 inch, 1 foot 1 yard and 1 mile. They are called 1 square inch, 1 square foot, 1 square yard and 1 square mile.

You must choose the size of square to suit the area you are measuring. Sometimes it is easy to see which square unit to use. Sometimes you have to change from one to another.

● What is a good size square to choose to work out how much carpet you need?

16

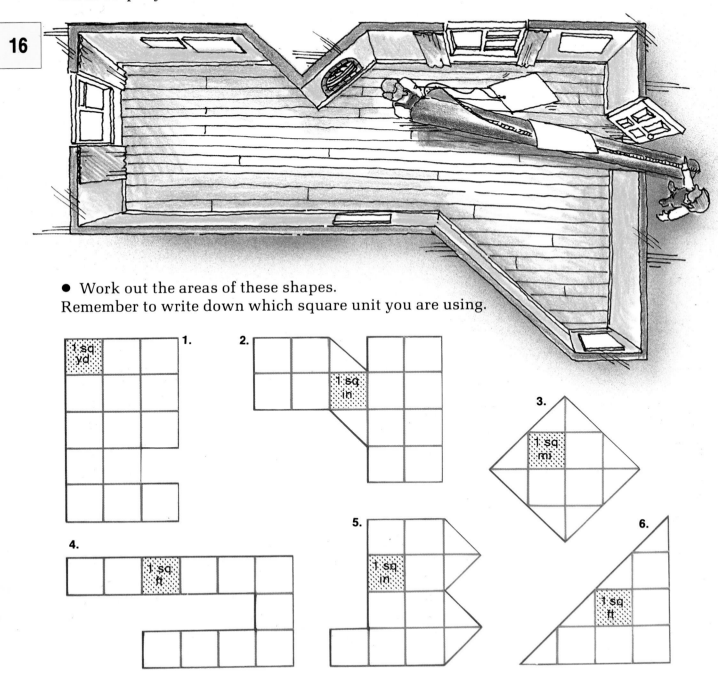

● Work out the areas of these shapes.
Remember to write down which square unit you are using.

Answers to puzzle 3 on page 13

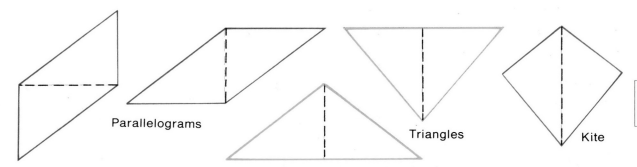

Parallelograms   Triangles   Kite

17

The area of each of the shapes stays the same as the area of the original rectangle.

Answers to page 14 investigation

These are the ten possibilities.

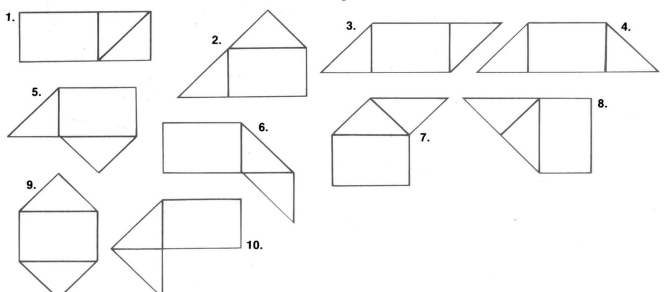

If you think you have found others, look carefully and see whether they are the same as one of these but rotated (turned around) or reflected (back to front or upside down).

The area of each of the shapes you can make is the same. The area of each of the combined shapes is the same as the areas of the three original shapes added together.

Answers to page 14 area puzzle

4 is the odd one out.

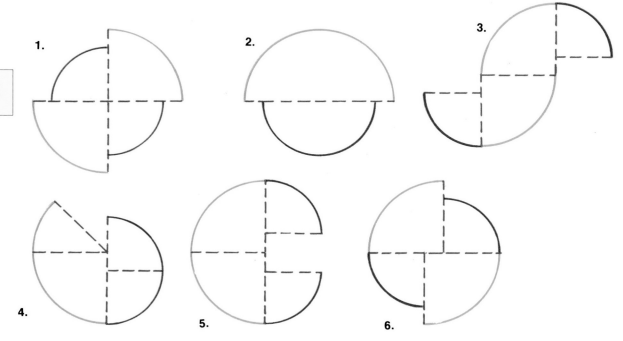

This puzzle was based on two different sized circles which were each cut up into four quarters. Experiment with shapes to make some area puzzles for your friends to solve.

- How much of each of these squares is shaded?

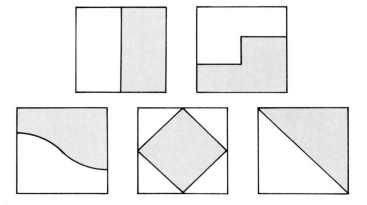

- What can you say about the areas of the shaded pieces?

Calculating the Area of Rectangles

How do you find the area of this **rectangle**

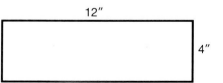

You can draw in all the square inches and count them. This will give you the correct answer, if you count carefully.

But suppose you had to find the area of the rectangle 112″ × 14″.

◇ Can you see an easier way?
Look again at the 12″ by 4″ rectangle.
There are four rows of square inches.

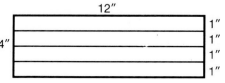

There are twelve square inches in each row.

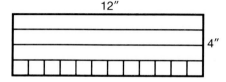

There are four rows of twelve square inches.
We can write this as the product 4 × 12 sq. in. = 48 sq.in.

● Use the same method to figure out how many square inches there are in the 112″ by 14″ rectangle.

● Try to find the areas of these rectangles without counting the squares. Remember, you must say what units you are using – square feet, square miles and so on.

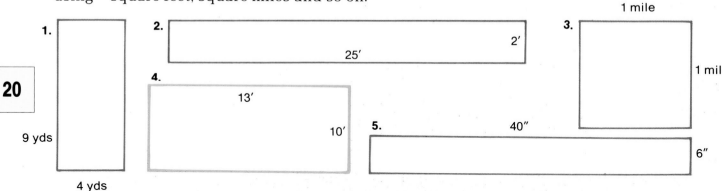

20

1. 9 yds / 4 yds

2. 25′ / 2′

3. 1 mile / 1 mil

4. 13′ / 10′

5. 40″ / 6″

Improving the Odds

At the school fair is a booth with a map of Treasure Island drawn on a grid of squares. Hidden under some of the squares are crosses indicating where the prizes are. For each turn that you buy, you are allowed to stick four squares on the map.

Each square must touch another at a corner but not at the sides.

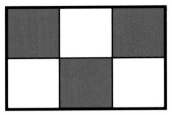

Allowed   Not allowed

The squares are then enclosed to form an area.

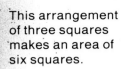

This arrangement of three squares makes an area of six squares.

If a square with a cross is within your area you win a prize.

● What is the best way of laying your four squares so that you have the greatest chance of winning a prize? What is the greatest number of squares you can enclose in an area?

● What is the worst way to arrange your squares if you want to win?

At the end of the afternoon there are still some unclaimed prizes. You are now allowed five squares a turn.

● What are the largest and smallest numbers of squares you can enclose this time?

● Can you predict the largest and smallest areas enclosed by six squares?

Answers to page 20

THE AREA OF A RECTANGLE = LENGTH × HEIGHT

You should have found the answers to the areas of the rectangles on page 20 by multiplying the length of each rectangle by its height. That is the same as multiplying the number of square units in a row by the number of rows in the rectangle.

22

1. 4 sq. yd. in a row, 9 rows   4 sq. yd. × 9 = 36 sq. yd.
2. 25 sq. ft. in a row, 2 rows   25 sq. ft. × 2 = 50 sq. ft.
3. 1 sq. mi. in a row, 1 row   1 sq. mi. × 1 = 1 sq. mi.
4. 13 sq. ft in a row, 10 rows   13 sq. ft. × 10 = 130 sq.ft.
5. 40 sq. in. in a row, 6 rows   40 sq.in. × 6 = 240 sq.in.

If you got these right, go on to page 23.
If you need more practice, try these.

Remember, decide on the units, and see how many squares are in the row and how many rows there are. Multiply squares times rows to find the total number of squares.

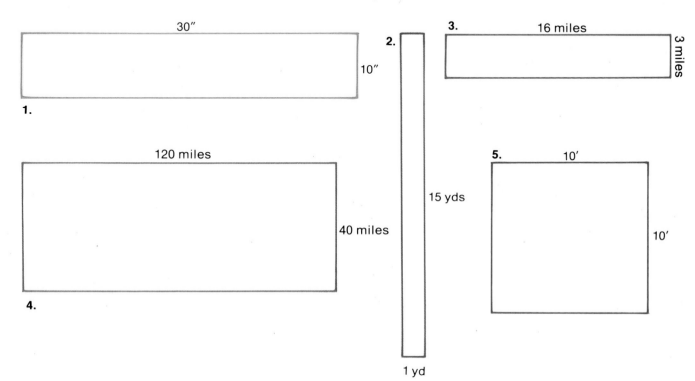

Harder examples with rectangles

Rectangle sides sometimes have measurements which include fractions of a unit. You can still use the same methods of working out the area. You can count up the whole squares and the parts of squares. Or you can multiply the length by the width. That is the same as multiplying the number of squares and part squares in a row by the number of rows and part rows.

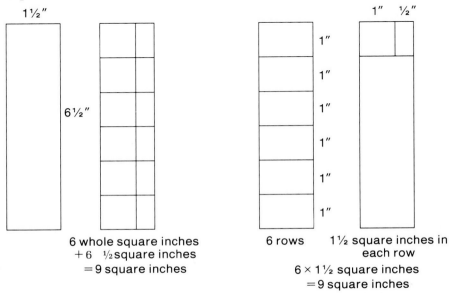

6 whole square inches
+ 6 ½ square inches
= 9 square inches

6 rows

1½ square inches in each row

6 × 1½ square inches
= 9 square inches

● How much glass do you need for this picture and the ones on the next page?

If you want to use a calculator to work out the multiplications, remember that $\frac{1}{2} = 0.5$ and $\frac{1}{4} = 0.25$.

1.

How many square inches in the rectangle?

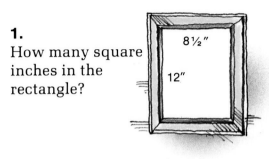

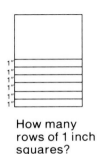

How many rows of 1 inch squares?

How many whole inches in a row?

How many part inch squares in a row?

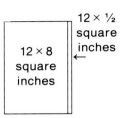

$12 \times 8\frac{1}{2}$ sq. in. = ?

$12 \times 8\frac{1}{2}$ is the same as

$(12 \times 8) + (12 \times \frac{1}{2})$

- The frames for the pictures are cut from lengths of wood. What length of wood do you need for each picture?

24

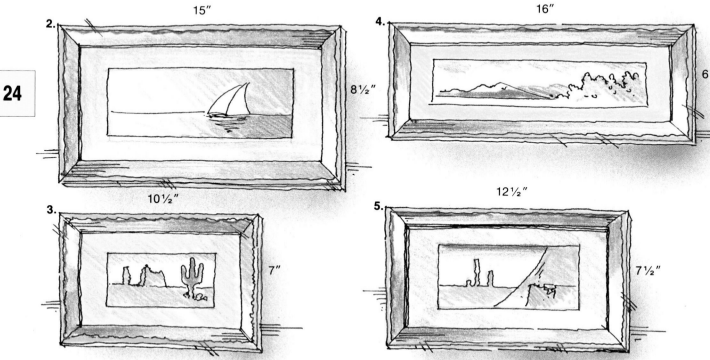

- You can arrange the pictures in order according to how much glass they need. Or you can arrange them according to how much wood they need. Does it make any difference?

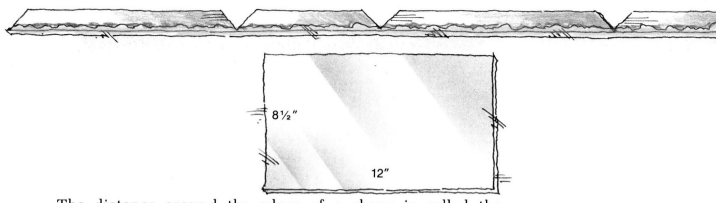

The distance around the edges of a shape is called the **perimeter**.

The glass covers the area of the picture. The frame goes around the perimeter.

Answers to improving the odds

To improve your chance of winning, you need to enclose the greatest number of squares possible.

The greatest possible area you can enclose with your 4 squares is 16 squares.

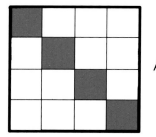

Area = 16

The worst way to arrange your squares, if you want to win, is to enclose the smallest number of squares possible.

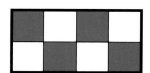

Area = 8

The minimum area you can enclose with four squares is eight squares.

These are some of the in between possibilities.

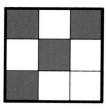 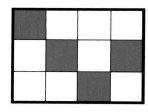 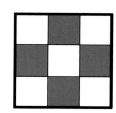

Area = 9   Area = 12   Area = 9

The largest and smallest areas you can enclose with 5 squares are 25 and 10 squares.

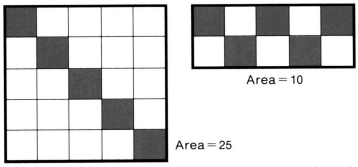

Area = 10

Area = 25

For 6 squares, the largest possible area enclosed is 36 squares and the smallest possible is 12 squares.

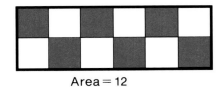

Area = 12

If we record these results in a table, the pattern becomes clear.

Table of Patterns		
Number of squares	**Largest Area**	**Smallest Area**
3	9 (3 × 3)	6 (3 × 2)
· 4	16 (4 × 4)	8 (4 × 2)
5	25 (? × ?)	10 (? × 2)
6	36 (? × ?)	12 (? × 2)

Once you have spotted the patterns, you can predict the answers for any number of squares.

Calculating the Areas of Parallelograms

A **parallelogram** is a four-sided shape with two pairs of straight, **parallel** sides. It is like a rectangle which has been pushed over.

This gives us a good clue about how to work out the area of a parallelogram.

You can see in these drawings that if you cut off one end of a parallelogram and move it to the other end, the parallelogram becomes a rectangle.

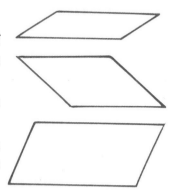

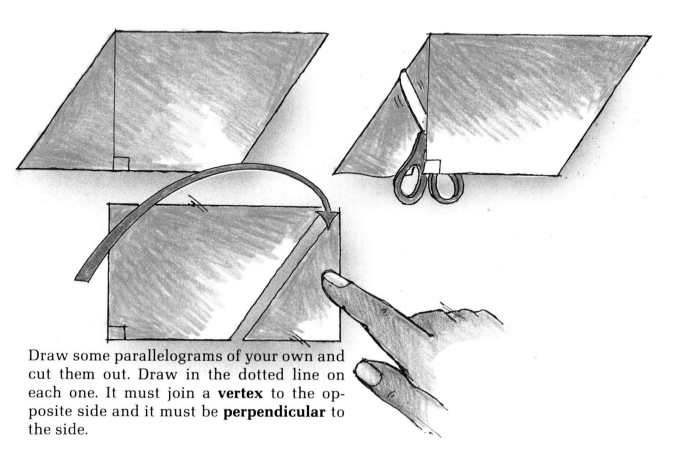

Draw some parallelograms of your own and cut them out. Draw in the dotted line on each one. It must join a **vertex** to the opposite side and it must be **perpendicular** to the side.

Cut along the dotted line. Move the cut off piece to the other end of the parallelogram. You now have a rectangle.

◇ How do you calculate the area of the rectangle you just made?

Look back at page 22 if you have forgotten.

28

Make sure that all your parallelograms can be turned into rectangles. Sometimes you may need to turn them around to see how to do it.

● What are the areas of these parallelograms?
Remember to state what unit squares you are using.

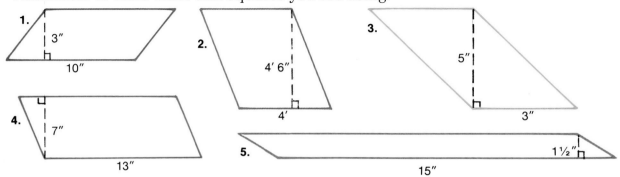

Because the sides of a parallelogram are parallel, the perpendicular distance between them is the same wherever you draw it.

With this parallelogram, you need to decide whether to use square feet or square inches.

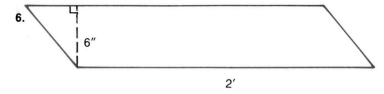

If you use square inches in number 6, there are 6 rows of 24 square inches in the equivalent rectangle. The parallelogram, therefore, has an area of 6 × 24 in. = 144 sq. in.

If you use square feet in the same example, there is half a row of two square feet in the equivalent rectangle. The area of the parallelogram is $\frac{1}{2}$ × 2 ft. = 1 sq. ft.

● The two answers to example 6 may surprise you. Do 144 square inches cover the same amount of space as a square foot?

Let us look more closely at a square with sides of 1 foot

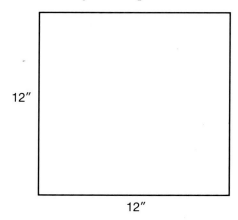

12″

12″

If we draw in the square inches which fit inside it, there will be twelve squares in a row.

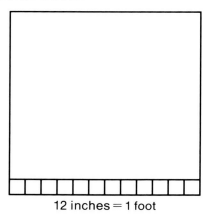

12 inches = 1 foot

● How many rows of twelve inch squares will it take to fill the whole foot square?

● How many inch squares does it take to fill a foot square?
● Work out the area of the parallelogram below, in square feet and in square inches.

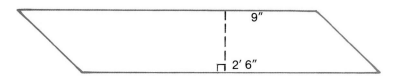

9″

2′ 6″

Have you learned how to calculate the area of a parallelogram? Here are some to practice on.

Remember, you need to know the length and the **perpendicular height**. You will need a ruler and a set square.

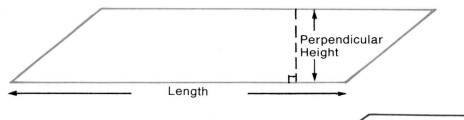

Sometimes you have to extend the base of the parallelogram to find the perpendicular height.

Although the area is the same whichever way you turn a parallelogram, it will make the calculations easier if you use the measurements of the sides marked "length" as the length.

● Find the area of the parallelograms below.

Check your answers on page 33.

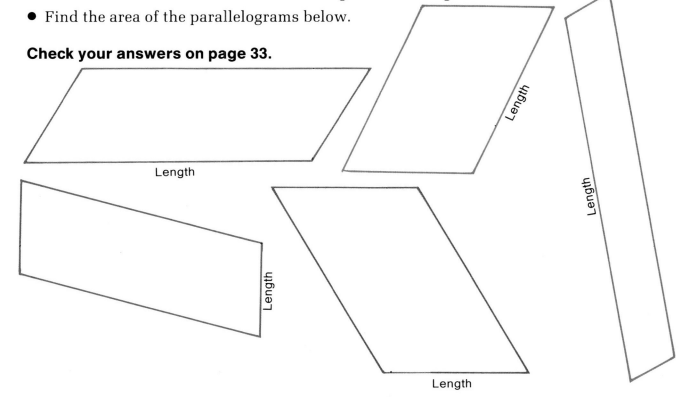

Panels and Pens

● How many different rectangular pens can the farmer make with 12 fence panels?

(A square is a rectangle – it is a rectangle with four equal sides.)

Cut 6 drinking straws in half to represent the 12 panels. Each piece of straw represents the top edge of a panel. You are making a plan of the pen.

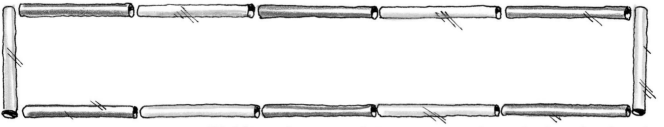

This way of arranging the panels gives an area of 5 squares

Divide each pen up into squares, where the length of each side of a square is the length of a panel. Use the squares to calculate the area of each pen the farmer can build.

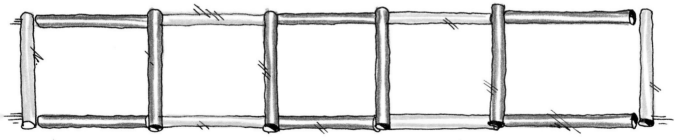

- What is the smallest area the farmer can enclose? What is the largest?

- What are the smallest and largest areas that the farmer can enclose with 14 panels?

- What happens if the farmer uses 13 panels?

- Experiment with different numbers of panels. Record your results. Notice especially what the smallest and largest areas are for each number of panels.

- What are the largest and smallest fields the farmer could make with 50 panels and with 100 panels?

Answers to calculating parallelogram areas

1. 3 in. × 1 in. = 3 sq. in.
2. 2 in. × $1\frac{1}{4}$ in. = $2\frac{1}{2}$ sq. in.
3. 4 in. × $\frac{1}{2}$ in. = 2 sq. in.
4. 1 in. × $2\frac{1}{2}$ in. = $2\frac{1}{2}$ sq. in.
5. $1\frac{1}{2}$ in. × 2 in. = 3 sq. in.

If you got these right, turn back to page 31.

If you are still unsure, the perpendiculars have been drawn in the diagrams for you and the measurements written in.

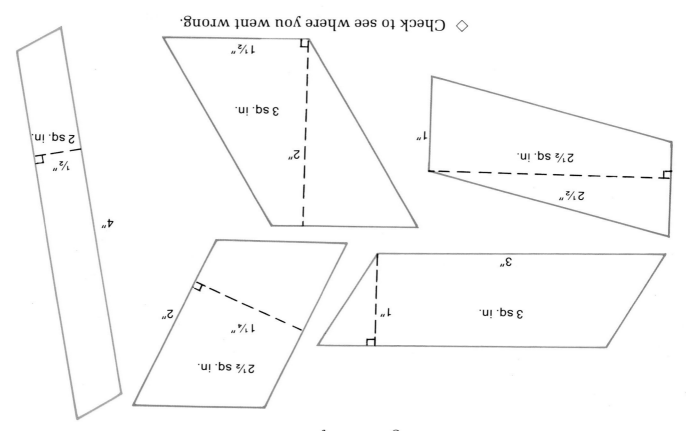

◇ Check to see where you went wrong.

Turn back to page 31.

Answers to panels and pens

These diagrams show the pens you can build with 12 panels.

One panel has been taken from the top and bottom and added to the sides of the field each time. It is a good idea to make up a system like this. It helps you to spot all the possibilities.

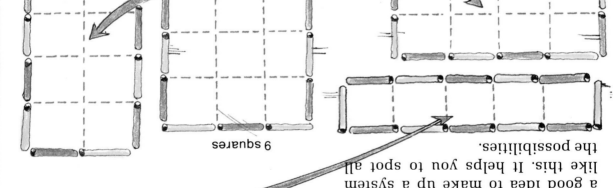
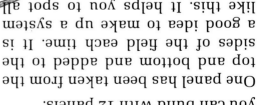

5 squares

9 squares

8 squares

These are the results for 14 fence panels.

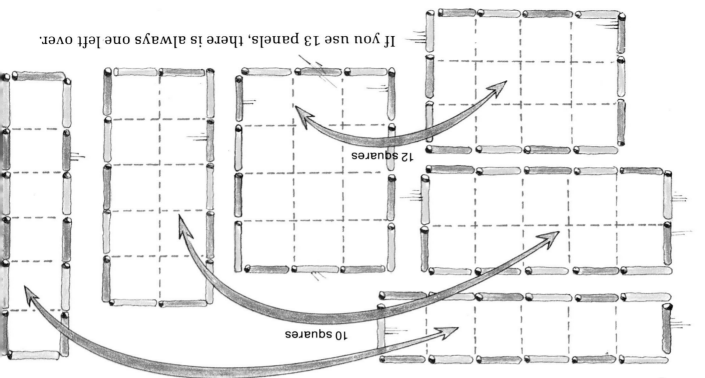

6 squares

10 squares

12 squares

If you use 13 panels, there is always one left over.

The smallest area

If you look at the diagrams you can see that the long thin fields, with only one fence panel at each end, have the smallest area.

12 panels   smallest area = 5
14 panels   smallest area = 6

● What do you guess the smallest area would be for 16 panels?

Make a quick sketch to check.

● What is the smallest area for 50 panels?

12 panels   smallest area = 5
14 panels   smallest area = 6
16 panels   smallest area = 7
50 panels   smallest area = ?

● Look for the pattern building up, or imagine the shape of the pen in your mind's eye. You don't need to write out all the numbers between sixteen and fifty.

The largest area

It is a little more difficult to predict the largest number of squares made by a given number of panels.

You were probably not surprised to see that a square gives the largest area, if it is possible to make one with the panels. With 12 panels you can make a square. With 14 panels you cannot.

● How can you tell if a given number of panels will make a square? Remember a square has four equal sides.

- Can you make a square from 100 panels? Can you make a square from 50 panels?

- How do you find the maximum area when you cannot make a square?

If you look at the diagrams for 14 panels, you can see that the maximum areas come from getting as close to a square as possible.

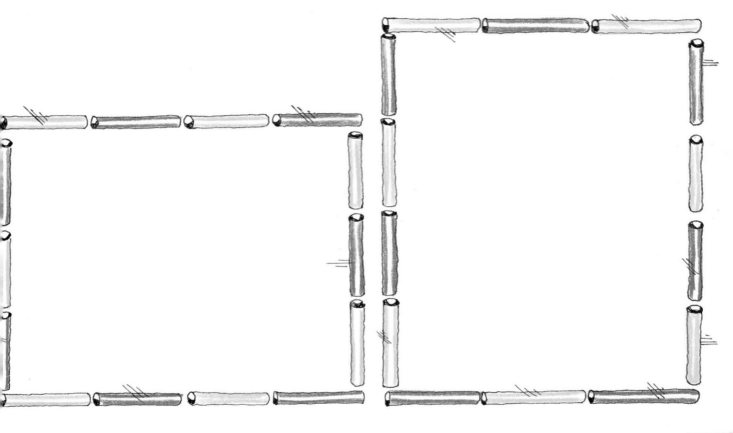

If you find two consecutive numbers which add up to half the number of panels, you have the shape you need. Try it with 18 panels. Draw a quick sketch to check.

You have all you need now to work out the largest area for 50 panels and 100 panels. You can work out the smallest and largest fields for any number of panels you like.

Calculating the Area of Triangles

You need scissors, glue, a set square and plenty of scrap paper. Draw five triangles. Make them as different from each other as you can. Here are some ideas to get you started.

Cut out your five triangles. Make a copy of each one, so that you have five pairs of triangles.

◇ Take one of each pair of triangles. Draw a **perpendicular** line from a **vertex** to the opposite side. A set square will help you. Cut along the line you just drew.

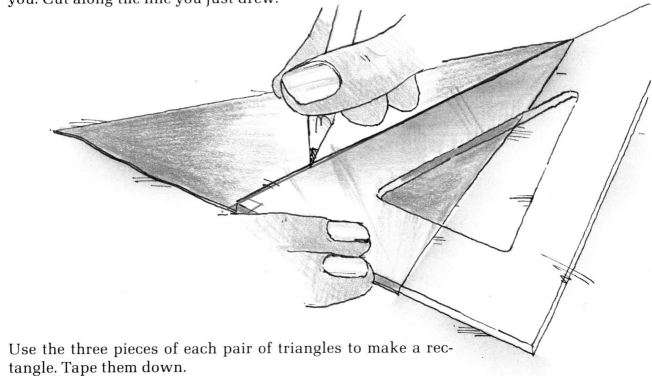

Use the three pieces of each pair of triangles to make a rectangle. Tape them down.

Area of rectangle =
Area of triangle **A** +
Area of triangle **B**

You now have five rectangles. Each rectangle is made from two identical triangles. In each case the area of one of the triangles must be half the area of the rectangle.

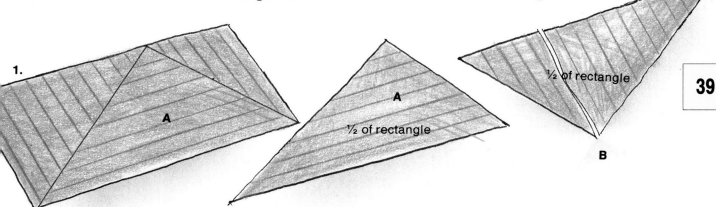

You know that to calculate the area of a rectangle, you multiply its length by its height.

Area of rectangle
= Length × height
= 2½″ × 1″
= 2½ sq. in.

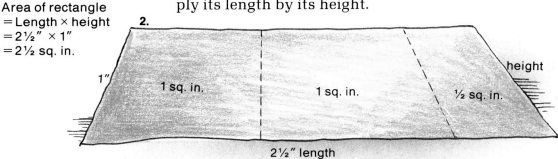

Look at your rectangles. You can see that the length of the rectangle is the same as the base of the triangle. The rectangle's height is the same as the triangle's perpendicular height.

Area of triangle
= ½ area of rectangle
= ½ × length × height of triangle
= ½ × 2½″ × 1″ = 1¼ sq. in.

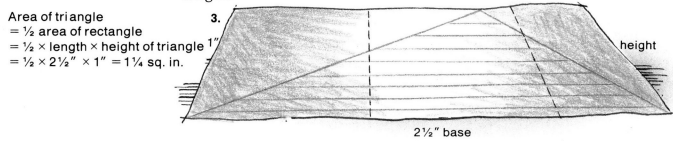

The area of the triangle is $\frac{1}{2}$ base × height

You can use this to find the area of any triangle.

What are the areas of
these triangles?

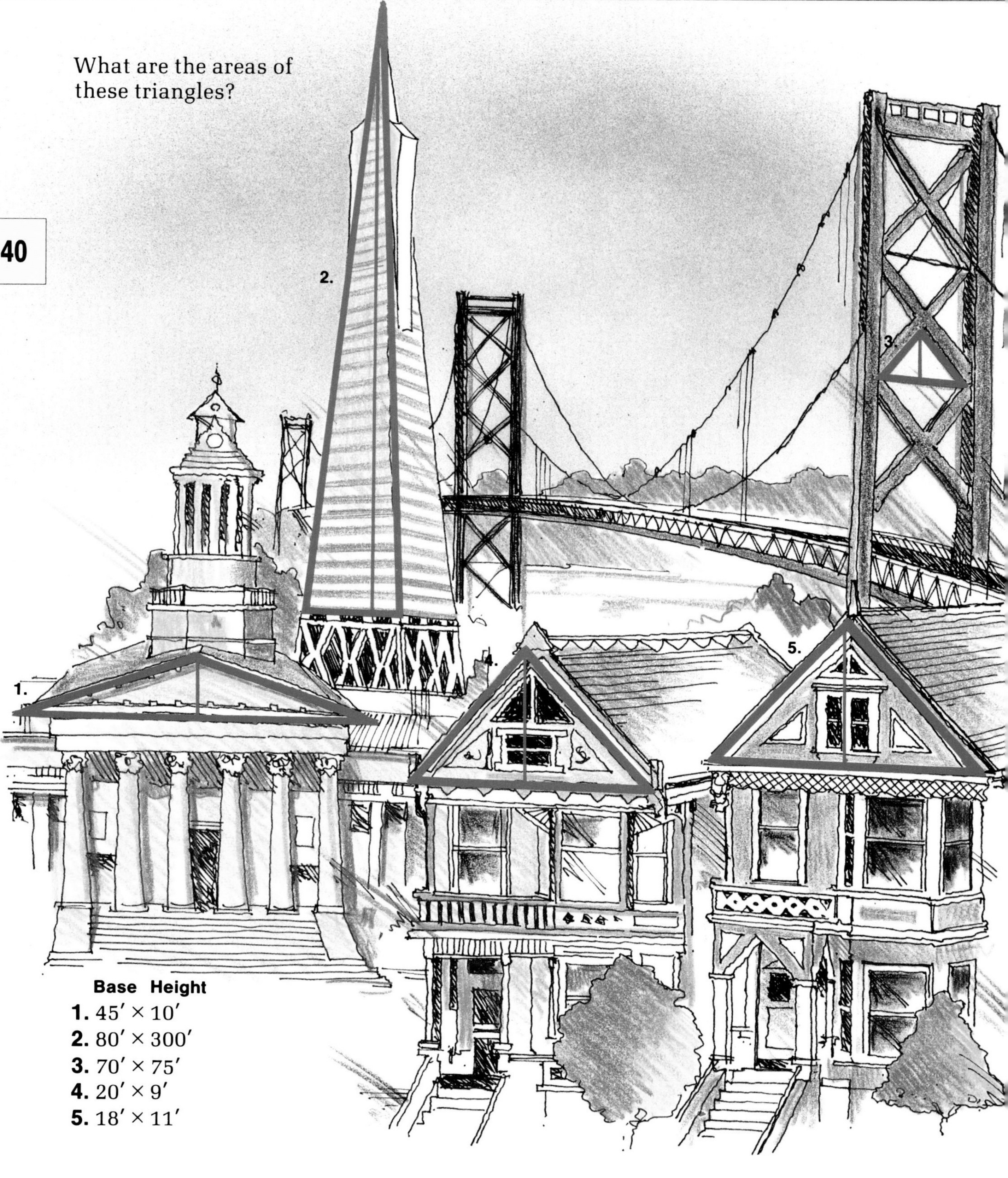

40

2.

3.

5.

1.

Base   Height
1. 45′ × 10′
2. 80′ × 300′
3. 70′ × 75′
4. 20′ × 9′
5. 18′ × 11′

Calculating the Area of Awkward Shapes

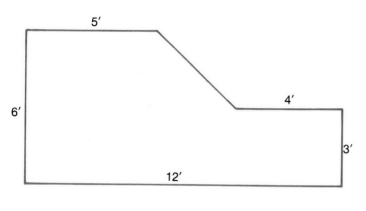

You can use your knowledge about the areas of rectangles, parallelograms and triangles to work out the area of any shape with straight lines. Sometimes all you need to do is divide the shape into pieces and then add the areas of the pieces together.

There are many ways you can split this shape to find its total area. This is one possibility.

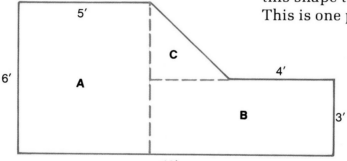

Area A × 5 ft. × 6 ft. = 30 sq. ft.
Area B × 7 ft. × 3 ft. = 21 sq. ft.
Area C × $\frac{1}{2}$ × 3 ft. × 3 ft. = $4\frac{1}{2}$ sq. ft.

Total area of shape = $55\frac{1}{2}$ sq. ft.

◇ Try working out the total area when the shape is cut up this way.

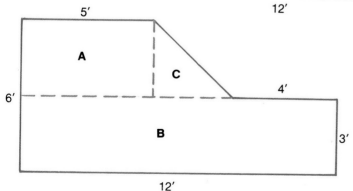

SupaSigns, Inc. makes plastic letters for shop signs. The price they charge their customers for each letter is worked out by calculating the area of the letter.

Calculate the areas of these letters. They are all 21″ tall and 3″ wide. The dotted lines show ways of splitting them into rectangles, parallelograms and triangles. You can split them your own way, if you prefer.

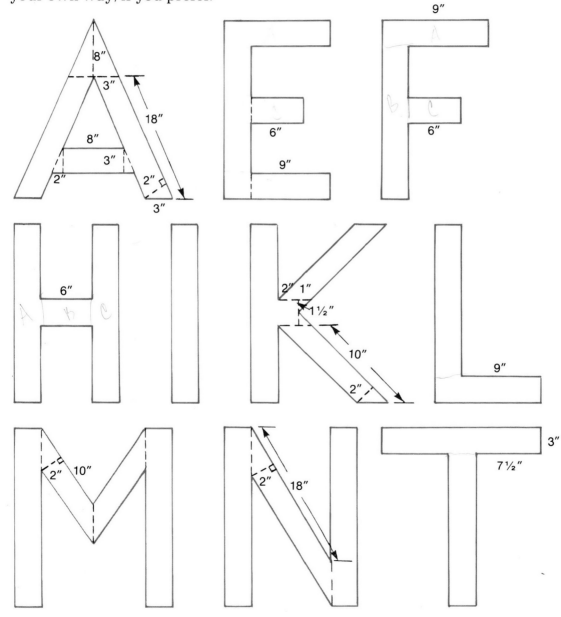

Kellie Filman wants a sign for her new sandwich shop. She has spent most of her money on furniture and equipment for the shop and needs to keep the cost of the sign as low as possible.

● If she buys from SupaSigns, Inc., which of these is the cheapest sign?

1. Kellie Filman's Sandwich Shop
2. Kellie's Sandwich Shop
3. Filman's Sandwich Shop

43

Some other odd shapes for you to try.

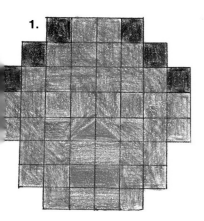

1.

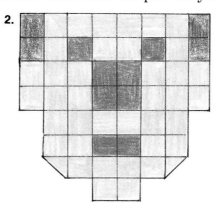

2.

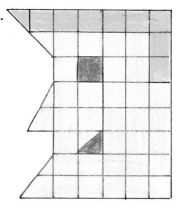

3.

Sometimes it is easier to subtract some of the area.

Suppose I wanted to know if I had enough paint to cover the wall of my house. I have only a quarter left of a gallon tin.

44

The easiest way is to calculate the total wall area and then subtract the areas of the window and the patio doors.

The paint covers at a rate of 700 square feet per gallon.

$$\text{Area of house} = 14 \text{ ft.} \times 11 \text{ ft.} + \tfrac{1}{2} \times 5 \text{ ft.} \times 11 \text{ ft.}$$
$$= 154 \text{ ft} + 27\tfrac{1}{2} \text{ ft.} = 181\tfrac{1}{2} \text{ sq. ft.}$$

Area of window $= 3 \text{ ft.} \times 2\tfrac{1}{2} \text{ ft.} = 7\tfrac{1}{2}$ sq. ft.
Area of patio door $= 6\tfrac{1}{2} \text{ ft.} \times 6\tfrac{1}{2} \text{ ft.} = 42\tfrac{1}{4}$ sq. ft.
Total area unpainted $= 49\tfrac{3}{4}$ sq. ft.

Total area to be painted $= 181\tfrac{1}{2}$ sq. ft. $- \ 49\tfrac{3}{4}$ sq. ft.
$= 131\tfrac{3}{4}$ sq. ft.

● Is there enough paint?

● How many square feet of flooring does Kellie need to buy for her shop?

One way to find out is to calculate the total floor area first. Then calculate the areas of the sinks, the refrigerated display, the built-in display and the counter. None of these need floor covering under them, so you can subtract their total area from the total floor area.

● Total floor area = ? ● Area under sinks = ?
● Area under refrigerator = ? ● Area under built-in display = ?
● Area under counter = ? ● Area under bar = ?

● Total area not needing flooring = ?
● Total area of flooring needed = ?

Filling Space

Building with boxes

Challenge

How many different **solids** can you build using three boxes of the same size? Empty match boxes or food cartons are ideal, as long as all three are the same size.

● How much space does each solid fill?

Counting in three dimensions

Stacking shelves

◇ How many cans of beans will these shelves hold?

You cannot see to count them because the back two rows are hidden. But you can see a front view and a side view. You can combine these to figure out the answer.

From the front you can see that there are three rows with eight cans in a row. This gives a display of twenty four cans. From the side you can see that the display is three rows deep. The shelves hold seventy two cans. 3 rows × 24 cans = 72 cans.

- How many cans do these shelves hold?

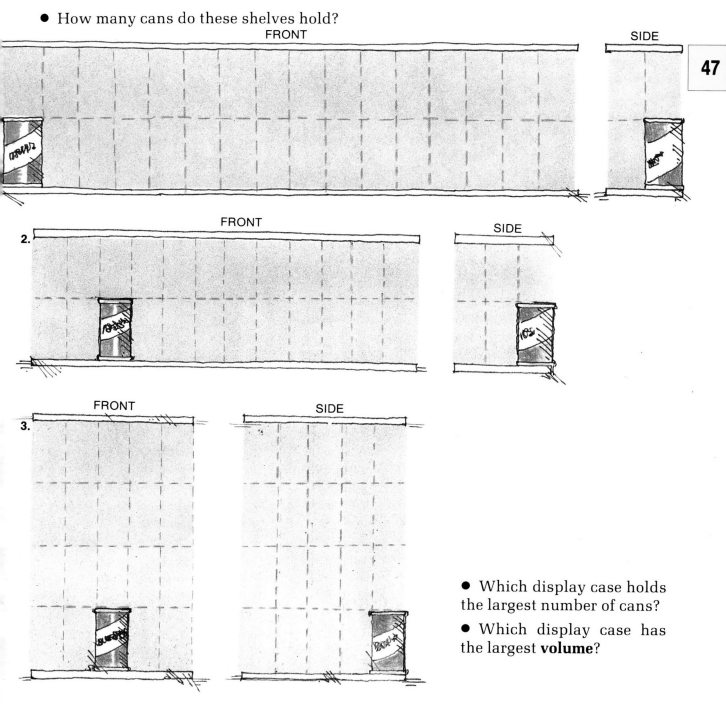

FRONT   SIDE

2. FRONT   SIDE

3. FRONT   SIDE

- Which display case holds the largest number of cans?

- Which display case has the largest **volume**?

These are some of the ways of building solids with three boxes. There are many more.

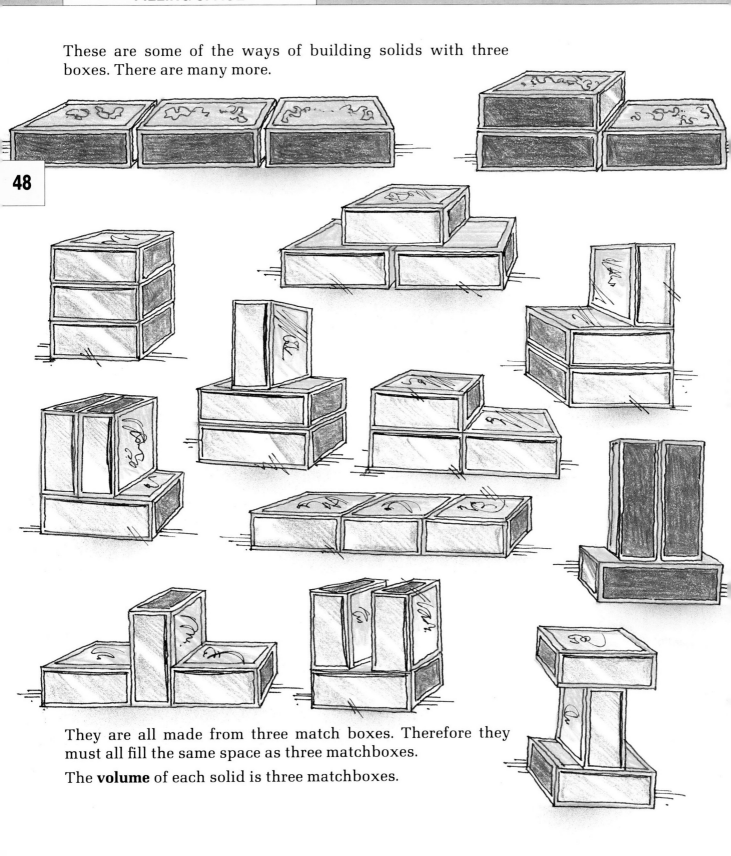

They are all made from three match boxes. Therefore they must all fill the same space as three matchboxes.

The **volume** of each solid is three matchboxes.

Answers

The answers to the cans questions are:
1. $8 \times 4 \times 2 = 64$ cans
2. $12 \times 2 \times 3 = 72$ cans
3. $5 \times 4 \times 5 = 100$ cans

The display case with the largest volume is number 3.

If you were right, go on to the next page.

Bricks in a wall

How many bricks are in
each of these walls?

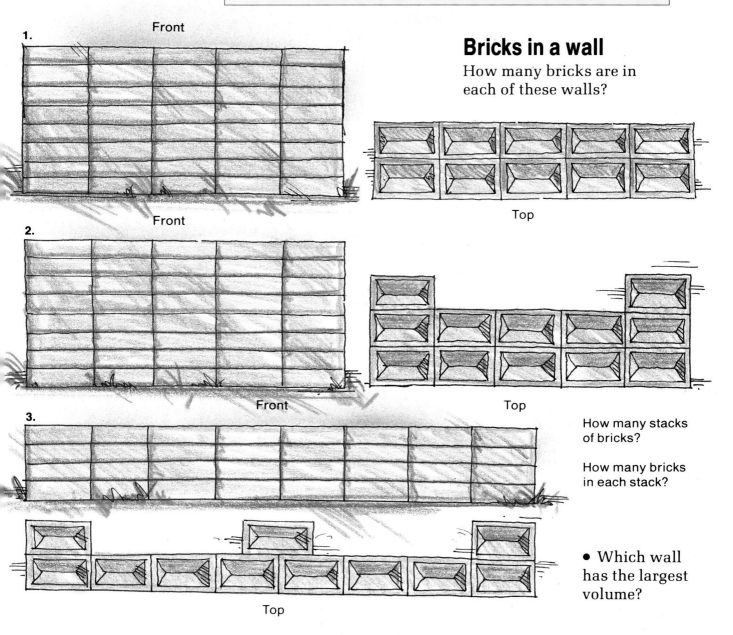

1.

Front

2.

Front

3.

Front

Top

Top

Top

How many stacks
of bricks?

How many bricks
in each stack?

● Which wall
has the largest
volume?

Boxes and Cubes

A **box** is a solid made up of rectangular sides whose edges meet at **right angles**.

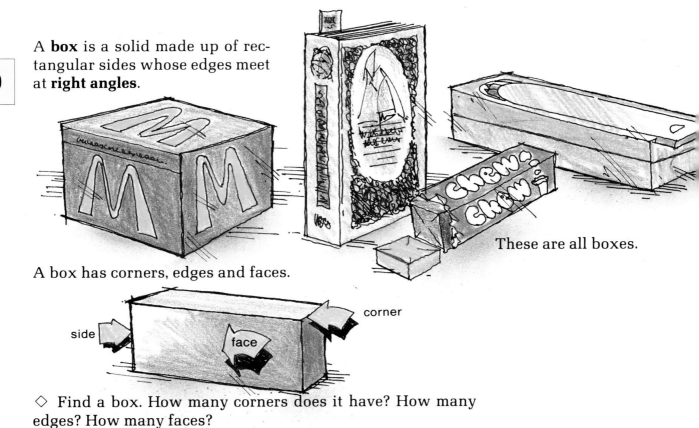

These are all boxes.

A box has corners, edges and faces.

side   face   corner

◇ Find a box. How many corners does it have? How many edges? How many faces?

A **cube** is a box with square faces.

● Which of these boxes are cubes?

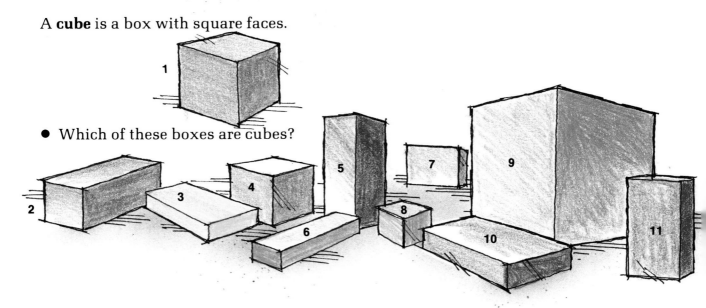

Filling space with cubes

Because they are made of straight sides which meet at **right angles**, cubes and boxes fill space without leaving any gaps. When we filled display cases with cylindrical cans, there were gaps around them which were filled with air. The display cases were not completely filled by the cans.

This makes cubes very useful when we want to measure volume.

51

● How many cubes are there in each of these animals?

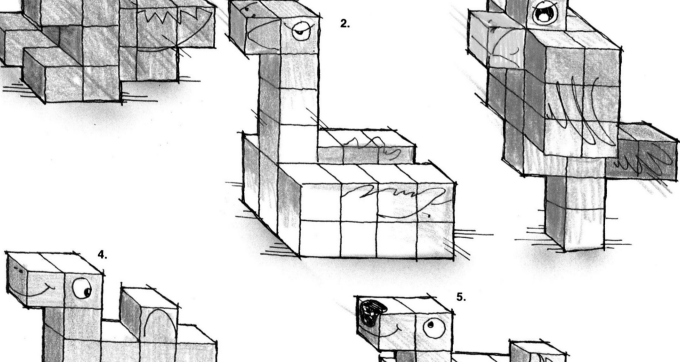

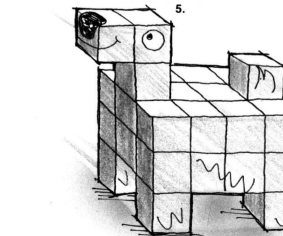

Calculating Volumes

Sometimes we can take short cuts in working out the number of cubes in a solid. Solids are built up in layers of cubes or parts of cubes. When every layer has the same number of cubes, we can multiply the number of cubes in one layer by the number of layers. This is the same method we used to count the cans and the bricks.

Calculating the volume of boxes

◇ How many building blocks fit into this box?

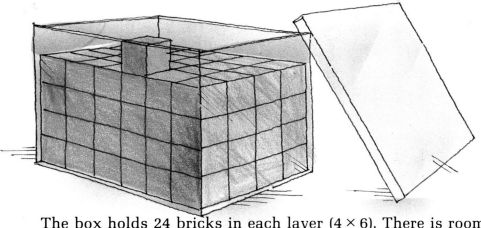

The box holds 24 bricks in each layer (4 × 6). There is room for five layers. The box holds 120 (24 × 5).

● Calculate the number of cubes in these solids.

First calculate the number of cubes in a layer. (Multiply the number of cubes in a row by the number of rows.) Then multiply the number of cubes in a layer by the number of layers.

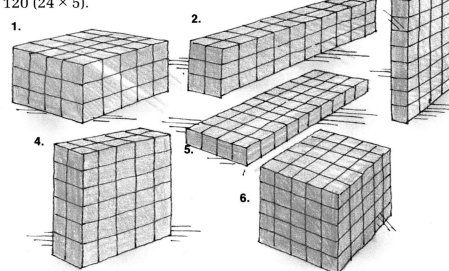

1.

2.

3.

4.

5.

6.

Prisms

Solids that are built up in layers which are all the same, are called **prisms**. Cuboids are prisms. A loaf of bread is a prism. It can be cut into slices which are all the same shape. So is a wedge of cheese.

A tomato is not a prism. Whichever way you slice it, you end up with different sized slices.

Sometimes the layers are built up side by side – the way we looked at the cans in the display case. Sometimes the layers build up from the bottom to the top – the way we calculated the bricks in the walls.

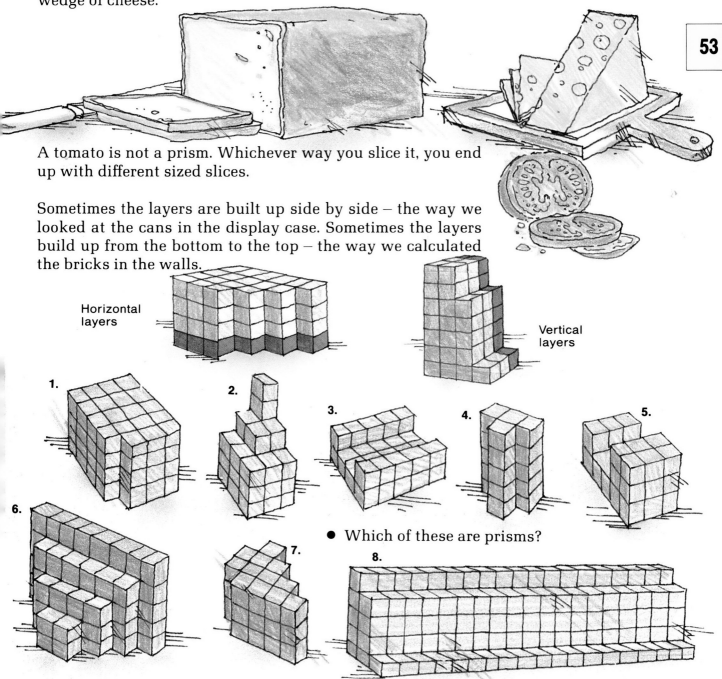

Horizontal layers

Vertical layers

1.

2.

3.

4.

5.

6.

7.

8.

● Which of these are prisms?

Answers to the number of cubes in the solids on page 52

1. 60 cubes **2.** 60 cubes **3.** 60 cubes
4. 60 cubes **5.** 40 cubes **6.** 125 cubes

> **If your answers were correct, go on to the investigation at the bottom of the page.**

How to work out the answers

There are 3 rows of 4 cubes in each layer. That is 12 cubes in each layer.

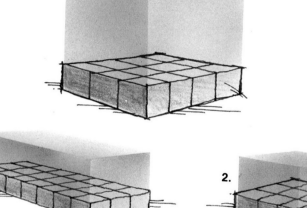

There are 5 layers. 5 layers each with 12 cubes gives a total of 60 cubes. 5 layers × 12 cubes = 60 cubes.

1. **2.**

Making sure

Calculate the number of cubes in these solids.

3.

Investigation

● How many different cuboids can you make from 16 cubes?

Here is one to get you started.
It is much easier to do this with some real cubes than to try to do it in your head. Sugar lumps or toy bricks will do.

4.

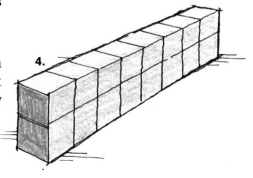

Answers to prisms questions on page 53

The solids were all prisms except 2 and 6.

Calculating the volume of prisms

We can use the same method we used to calculate the volume of a box to calculate the volume of any prism. Multiply the number of cubes in each layer by the number of layers.
The only snag is that we must make sure that we look at it the right way around. Some prisms are made up of layers on top of each other. Others have layers side by side.

The layers in this prism are on top of each other. There are 4 layers. There are 19 cubes in each layer. The number of cubes in the prism = 4 × 19 = 76.

In this prism the layers are side by side. There are 3 layers. Each layer has 12 cubes. The number of cubes in the prism = 3 × 12 = 36.

● Calculate the number of cubes in these prisms.

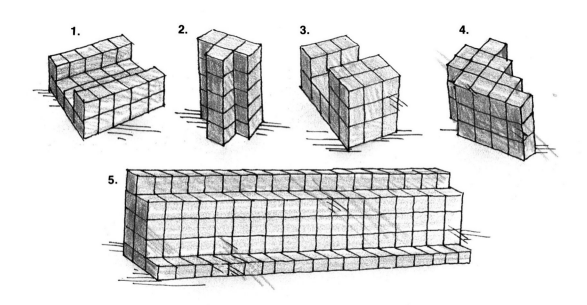

1.

2.

3.

4.

5.

Unit Cubes

Just as we could take sheets of newspaper to the carpet shop to explain how much carpet we wish to buy, so we could carry around heaps of wooden or cardboard blocks to show how big an oil tank we need, or how much concrete we need to cover the drive to a depth of six inches.

Obviously this is not very practical! The solution is to agree on a system of unit cubes to measure volume, just as we have unit squares to measure area.

The unit cubes are:

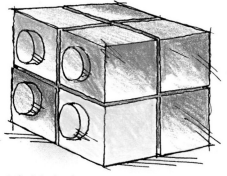

1 Cubic Inch
We do not use cubic inches very often. These eight modeling blocks make up a cubic inch. Each one is $\frac{1}{8}$ cu. in.

Cubic Feet
You need to know how many cubic feet are in your room to work out how powerful a heater you need.

Cubic Yards
Ready-mixed concrete is sold by the cubic yard. You have to calculate how much you will need.

Calculating volumes without drawing cubes

There is no need to fill up a solid with actual cubes. We can use the dimensions of the solid to calculate the volume.

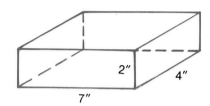

Although the one inch cubes that would fill this cuboid are not drawn in, we know how many there would be. There would be four rows of seven in each layer. There would be two layers. The total number of cubic inches of the box is: $4 \times 7 \times 2 = 56$.

● Calculate the volumes of these boxes.

1. There are six layers. How many cubes in each layer? What is the volume?

2. There are 120 cubes in each layer. How many layers are there? What is the volume?

3. How many layers? How many cubes in each layer?

4. Which three numbers do you need to multiply here to find the volume?

5. In the final example, you must decide which units to use. If you decide to use cubic feet, you must change the yards and inches to feet.

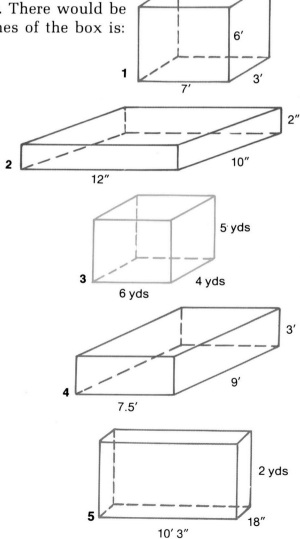

We can use the same method to work out the volume of any prism. Calculate the number of cubes in one layer and then multiply by the number of layers.

The layers in the prism are side by side. Each layer is made of two squares. The sum of the cubic inches in each layer is $(3 \times 3) + (2 \times 2) = 9 + 4 = 13$. There are 4 layers of cubic inches. The volume of the prism is $4 \times 13 = 52$ cu. in.

● Some for you to try.

1. Which way do the layers fit? How many cubic feet in each layer? How many layers?

2. If you looked down on the prism, the top would look like **2a**.
How many cubes in one layer? How many layers of cubes?

What is the volume?

3. In this example, you need to subtract an area to find the number of cubes in each layer.

Investigation

If you have a piece of cardboard, you can make a box without a lid. You cut out the corners, fold up the sides and join them with tape.

● Suppose you have a piece of cardboard which is 6″ square. If you want the box to have the maximum volume possible, what size corners should you cut out? Give your answer to the nearest $\frac{1}{4}''$

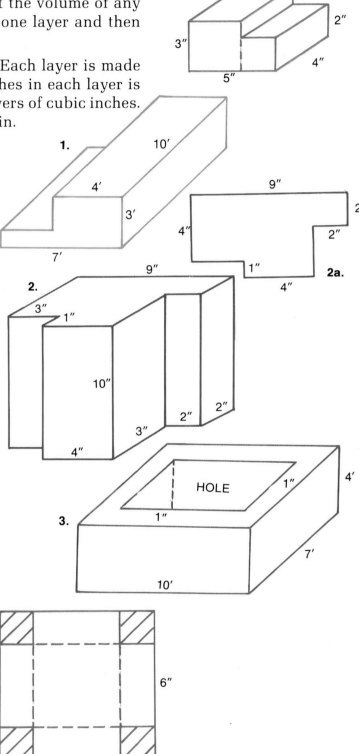

Surface Area and Volume

Look at these two cubes.

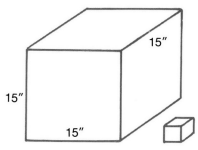

The 1 inch cube has a total surface area of 6 square inches. It has 6 faces. Each face has an area of 1 square inch.

It has a volume of 1 cubic inch.

For the 1 inch cube
$$\frac{\text{area}}{\text{volume}} = \frac{6}{1} = 6$$

The 15 inch cube has a total surface area of 1,350 square inches. Each face has an area of 225 square inches.
$$6 \times 225 = 1,350$$

It has a volume of 3,375 cubic inches.
(15 in. × 15 in. × 15 in. = 3,375 cu. in.)

For the 15 inch cube
$$\frac{\text{area}}{\text{volume}} = \frac{1,350}{3,375} = 0.4$$

Animals are always losing heat through their skins. They eat to make energy. If they have large bodies, they make a lot of heat. If they have small bodies, they lose, through their skins, a high proportion of the energy provided by the food they eat. You could think of a mouse as a 1 inch cube and a child as a 15 inch cube.

The mouse has to keep eating because it has a large surface area in proportion to its volume. Each day, a mouse has to eat as much food as half its body weight just to stay alive.

Small animals find it difficult to live in very cold climates because they have a large surface area **in proportion to** their volume. Polar bears, which are large animals with thick coats, can survive where a mouse could not.

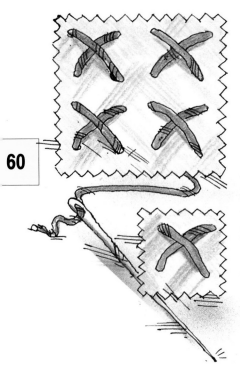

Enlargement and Area and Volume

A tapestry is being worked at 10 stitches to the inch. It is 3 feet long and 2 feet wide. 86,400 stitches are required to complete it. (360 × 240)

How many stitches does it take to fill a tapestry which is 6 feet long and 4 feet wide?

The answer is NOT 2 × 86,400.
It is 720 × 480 = 345,600 stitches. This is **4** x 86,400.

Look more closely.
In a 1 inch square of the tapestry, there is 1 cross stitch.

In a 2 inch square, there are four stitches.

When the lengths of the sides of the square are multiplied by 2, the number of stitches is multiplied by 4.

◇ Try it with a 3 inch square and a 6 inch square. Draw the squares and fill them with crosses, if you need to make sure.

A cassette storage unit, 8 inches long, 3 inches deep and 5 inches high, holds 10 cassettes. How many cassettes does a unit 16 inches long, 6 inches deep and 10 inches high hold?

Multiplying each of the dimensions by 2 makes the volume increase **8** times.

This box holds 60 bricks.

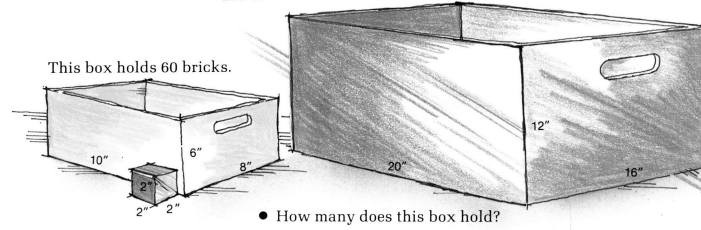

● How many does this box hold?

Glossary

adjacent next to

area the amount of surface an object covers

box a solid formed from six rectangles whose edges meet at right angles

cube a solid formed of six squares whose edges meet at right angles

diagonal a line joining two non-adjacent vertices of a shape

hexagon a closed shape with six straight sides. A closed shape has no gaps around its edge.

parallel lines that are parallel always remain the same distance apart. They will never meet, however far they extend.

parallelogram a four-sided shape with two pairs of parallel sides

perimeter the distance around the edges of a shape

perpendicular one line is perpendicular to another when they meet at a right angle (90 degrees)

prism a solid that has a uniform cross section. An unsharpened pencil is a prism; an ice cream cone is not.

rectangle a four sided shape with four right angles and two pairs of equal sides

rhombus a four sided shape in which all the sides are equal

right angle an angle of 90 degrees; a quarter turn

shape a two dimensional figure

solid a three dimensional figure

vertex the point where the edges of a shape or solid meet

volume the amount of space an object fills

Answers

Page 7
See page 8.

Page 10
Exact numbers vary, depending on how you align the grids. The table below will be useful as a guide.

Pool	Dots (including on edge)	Whole Shapes	Whole + more than ½ shapes
A	25 3	18	18 14
B	19 5	13	13 18
C	28 10	27	27 15
D	20 4	14	14 15

In this case, the method you use to compare the areas does not make any difference to the results. The third method is usually the most accurate.

Page 11
The most expensive patio is number 6 (36 slabs). The cheapest is number 3 (21 slabs).

Page 12
1. 30 slabs, $30 \times \$40 = \$1,200$
2. 25 slabs, $25 \times \$40 = \$1,000$
3. 21 slabs, $21 \times \$40 = \$840$
4. 24 slabs, $24 \times \$40 = \$960$
5. 31 slabs, $31 \times \$40 = \$1,240$
6. 36 slabs, $36 \times \$40 = \$1,440$
7. 35 slabs, $35 \times \$40 = \$1,400$

The quilt for a single bed costs $16 \times \$20 = \$320$.
The king size costs $24 \times \$20 = \$480$

Page 13
1. All the shapes have the same area – 10 squares.
2. The area of the two cut pieces stays the same as the area of the square, however you arrange them.
3. See page 17.

Page 14
See pages 17 and 18.

Page 16
Carpet is usually calculated in square yards.
1. 14 sq. yd. 2. 14 sq. in. 3. 8 sq. miles
4. 11 sq. ft. 5. 11 sq. in. 6. 8 sq. ft.

Page 18
In each case, one half of the square is shaded. The area of the shaded pieces in each diagram is the same

Page 19
There are 14 rows.
There are 112 in. in each row.
There are 14×112 in. $= 1,568$ sq. in.

Page 20
See page 22.

Page 21
See page 25-6

Page 22
1. 30 in. $\times$ 10 in. $= 300$ sq. in.
2. 1 yd. $\times$ 15 yd. $= 15$ sq. yd.
3. 16 miles $\times$ 3 miles $= 48$ sq. miles
4. 120 miles $\times$ 40 miles $= 4,800$ sq. miles
5. 10 ft. x 10 ft. $= 100$ sq. ft.

Pages 23 & 24
Glass required
1. $12 \times 8\frac{1}{2}$ in. $= 102$ sq. in.
2. $8\frac{1}{2} \times 15$ in. $= 127\frac{1}{2}$ (127.5) sq. in.
3. $7 \times 10\frac{1}{2}$ in. $= 73\frac{1}{2}$ (73.5) sq. in.
4. $6\frac{1}{4} \times 16$ in. $= 100$ sq.in.
5. $7\frac{1}{2} \times 12\frac{1}{2}$ in. $= 93\frac{3}{4}$ (93.75) sq. in.

Wood required for frame
1. 41 in. 2. 47 in. 3. 35 in. 4. 44.5 in. 5. 40 in.
(If you were really making picture frames, you would have to make an additional allowance for cutting the mitre joints of about 4".)
Number 4 is second in perimeter, but third in area

Page 26
To work out the maximum area, multiply the number of squares by itself. To work out the minimum area, multiply the number of squares by two.

Page 28
1. 10in. $\times$ 3 in. $= 30$ sq. in.
2. 4 ft. $\times$ 4$\frac{1}{2}$ ft. $= 18$ sq. ft.
3. 3 in. $\times$ 5 in. $= 15$ sq. in.
4. 13 in. $\times$ 7 in. $= 91$ sq. in.
5. 15 ft. $\times$ 1$\frac{1}{2}$ ft. $= 22\frac{1}{2}$ sq. ft.

Page 29
It takes 12 rows, which is 144 inch squares.
30 in. × 9 in. = 270 sq. in.
$\frac{3}{4}$ ft. × $2\frac{1}{2}$ ft. = $1\frac{7}{8}$ sq. ft. or
0.75 ft. × 2.5 ft. = 1.875 sq. ft

Page 32
See page 34.

Page 35
50 panels, smallest area = 24
(halve the number of panels, then subtract 1)
If the number of panels divides exactly by four, then they will make a square.

Page 36
You can make a square from 100 panels but not from 50.
The biggest area for 50 panels is 12 × 13 = 156 squares.
The largest area for 100 panels is 25 × 25 = 625 squares.

Page 40
1. 225 sq. ft. 2. 12,000 sq. ft. 3. 2,265 sq. ft.
4. 90 sq. ft. 5. 99 sq. ft.

Page 42
A = 126 sq.in. E = 135 sq.in. F = 108 sq.in. H = 144 sq. in. I = 63 sq. in. K = $110\frac{1}{2}$ sq. in. L = 90 sq. in. M = 166 sq. in. N = 162 sq. in. T = 108 sq. in.

Page 43
KELLIE'S SANDWICH SHOP is the cheapest sign.
The letters that are different are FMAN in Filman and KELE in Kellie.
1. 50 squares 2. 51 squares 3. 44 squares

Page 44
Yes, there is enough paint.

Page 45
Total area = 810 sq. ft.
Area under refrigerator = 36 sq. ft.
Area under counter = 45 sq. ft.
Area under sinks = 18 sq. ft.
Area under built-in display = 18 sq. ft.
Area under bar = 54 sq. ft.
Total = 171 sq. ft.
Total area of flooring needed = 639 sq. ft.

Page 46
See page 48.

Page 47
See page 49.

Page 49
1. 5 × 2 × 8 = 80 bricks
2. 8 courses of 12 bricks = 96 bricks
3. 4 courses of 11 bricks = 44 bricks
Wall 2 has the largest number of bricks and therefore the largest volume.

Page 50
A box has 8 corners, 12 edges and 6 faces.
1, 4, 8 and 9 are cubes.

Page 51
1. 27 2. 23 3. 26 4. 27 5. 32

Page 52
See page 54.

Page 53
See page 55.

Page 54
1. 63 cubes 2. 27 cubes 3. 81 cubes

Investigation
There are 3 other boxes you can make from 16 cubes: 16 × 1 × 1; 4 × 4 × 1; 4 × 2 × 2.

Page 55
1. 30 cubes 2. 20 cubes 3. 30 cubes 4. 36 cubes
5. 190 cubes

Page 57
1. 126 cu. ft. 2. 240 cu. in. 3. 120 cu. yds.
4. 202.5 cu. ft. 5. 92.25 cu. ft.

Page 58
1. 150 cu. ft. 2. 360 cu. in. 3. 30 cu. ft.

Investigation
Corners of 1″ square cut off give you a box with a volume of 16 cu. in. Increasing the size of the corners decreases the volume.

Page 60
The cassette unit will hold 80 cassettes.
The larger box will hold 8 × 60 = 480 bricks

63

Index

animals 59

bean cans 46-7
boxes 46, 48, 52, 58, 60
bricks 48-9
builder 11-12

cans 46-7
carpet 15, 16, 56
cassettes 60
circles 14, 18
counting 8
cubes 50-2, 54, 58, 59
cubic feet 56, 57, 58
cubic inches 56
cubic yards 56
cuboid 50-2, 54

dots 8-9, 15

enlargement 60
estimates 7-8, 11

farmer 31-2
fields 32

glass 15, 23-4
grid 10, 20

hardware store 7
hexagons 12, 15
Hexaquilts 12
house 44

Kellie Filman 43, 45
kite 17

matchboxes 46, 48
mosaic 15

newspaper 15, 56

paint 44
panels 31-2, 34-6
parallel 27-8
parallelogram 17, 27-30, 33,
    41
patterns 26
patio 11-2
paving slabs 12, 15
pens 31, 34-6
perimeter 24
perpendicular 27, 28, 29, 33,
    38
pictures 23-4
pools 8-10
prisms 53-5, 58

rectangle 13, 15, 20, 22-4, 39,
    41
reflection 17
rhombus 9-10, 15
right angles 50-1
rotation 17

shelves 46
slabs 12, 15
solids 46, 48, 52. 54
squares 12, 13, 15, 18, 20-1,
    25-6, 31, 35
square foot 15, 28, 29
square inch 15, 22-3, 28, 29
square mile 15
square units 15-6
square yard 15
store 7, 15
straws 31, 34-6
SupaSigns 42-3

tapestry 60
transparent grid 10
Treasure Island 20
triangle 13, 15, 17, 37-40, 41

units 15
unit cubes 56-8
unit squares 15-6

vertex 27, 38